MATEO LEARNS TO LOVE HIMSELF

MATEO LEARNS TO LOVE HIMSELF

learning self-love

AMARI SMITH
God

self_love_guru

CONTENTS

Dedication vi

chapter ix

One

1

About The Author 4

Dedication page

This book is dedicated to all my readers. This is my ninth published book, and I really appreciate everyone who decided to purchase it. Choosing self-love every day is not something that it is easy. But that is necessary. Especially for our children you look into the eyes of your kids every day, and you understand something clearly at last of them being joyful and happy as a kid. that is the light that I want to continue to see. but with that light, I want them to be able to choose certain actions that are loving towards themselves instead of sticking around a friend that necessarily is not the best for them just so that they can have friends or having boundaries, but not respecting those boundaries because they care so much about the person and not enough about themselves. I want everyone that reads my books to understand that this is something that I believe in so strongly that I feel like it is my obligation to share it with other people. There are many more books to come and I hope that I have consistent readers that stick along with me in this journey. I am blessed and I appreciate you and thank you every step of the way. I strongly believe that if you are a good person or good intentions everything in life is going to work out for you. And when you instill these good intentions and how to be a good person and how to accurately assess your emotions and how not to overly express your emotions you in turn make a good person out of a child. Caring more about others, then yourself can be very damaging no matter how good the intentions are. Therefore, self-love is so important and self-love is tied into so many concepts in life. Which you will see in every single new book that I write. I learned a lot on my journey and I want everyone to start their self-love journey. This has changed me completely for the better. Every person has a purpose on this earth. And I want everyone to find that purpose and the way you find your purpose is through self-love everything ties back to self-love. Therefore, self-love means everything thank you again for reading and never forget to choose peace and happiness for yourself.

CHAPTER ONE

Mateo has two sisters.

One mommy and one pet

He was the only mister

Mateo went to school

He usually sat alone

Until one day he met this girl named Jewel

Jewel became his best friend

They did everything together

Mateo Hoped it would never end

One day at school someone told Jewel, that Mateo was a loser.

Jewel was not sure how to feel.

She went along with it and threw Mateo into the pool.

Mateo went home and told his mommy

His mommy was upset, but told him this. We are going to talk to my friend Tommy.

Tommy told Mateo that some friends are not always meant to stay in your life.

This is why we must learn selflove

After hearing that Mateo was happy.

He went to school the next day and sat alone again

This time he wasn't Unhappy.

D d
D d

What I feel like, describes me best would be that I am a good person with genuine Intentions. But what I feel like describes me even better is my Instagram page here are a few captions:

self_love_guru7
This was so fresh and tasted so different◈. #vegan #healthylifestyle #god #peace #selflove #happiness #◈ #◈ #world #growth
self_love_guru7
Let it ride. Everything that has happened in the past happened that's it. Let it go!. Forgive who ever or whatever it is. Hate no one. So your happy can continue in the
present #self-love #peace #god #happiness #◈ #vegan #follow
self_love_guru7
Being honest is something that needs to be valued if you want to hear it or not. Use it to improve. Only someone who cares enough to say something is an amazing person to have by your side. Living in ignorance about something that you can improve on all because you don't want to hear it is
pathetic. #selflove #improvement #worth #postivity #fitnessmotivation #mindset #honesty #god
self_love_guru7
This is true. Extend your kindness once. You can't control someone life especially sense you've never walked a day in their shoes #selflove #happiness #peace #postivity #god
self_love_guru7
Hurt people ,hurt people is the worst popular quote possible because it's like it's giving you an excuse to be a bad person just because something bad happened in your day. You still be kind to people because they are not the people that hurt you. Or had anything to do with it. Hurt people that hurt other people are people that have not healed or tried to

heal from what is ailing them. That is a lazy thing to do heal instead #heal #happiness #peace #god #follow #selflove #postivity #knowyourworth #hurtpeoplehurtpeople

self_love_guru7
This is what not to do. When you have explained your hurt to someone and they hurt you as well. They have let you know that they don't respect,care, appreciate, value, or anything you else you need from someone that you have any kind of relationship with. You should be able to tell someone that they hurt and they change the behavior if they care. Start leaving instead of wasting time with someone that doesn't care about you. You are valuable and so is your time ❤◇. You are just talking to the wrong person. Have a good day everyone◇. #peace #choosejoy #god #selflove #happiness #follow

self_love_guru7
Eat or drink something healthy today◇❤◇◇. #peace #selflove #god #happiness #you

self_love_guru7
This is so beautiful. And he is speaking from a very deep place. When you want growth that is going to change your life or change who you are. You have to be able to give to others. It's amazing what lessons can do to a person they can really make you a whole completely different person. Change is not always a bad thing is usually a good thing embrace it. #selflove #peace #happiness #growth #god #give

self_love_guru7
Amazing attitude!!!. Love the positivity! I hope everyone is having a great day◇. #selflove #love #healthylifestyle #happiness #growth #❤

self_love_guru7
Everything can't stay bad all the time. I feel like it definitely depends on the person and how they look

at it. That doesn't mean that you won't cry one day to alleviate the pressure. But that does mean is that you will have a new skill that you did not have before. Learn to look at things a different way sometimes And also evaluate if it's worth it. Because sometimes I can say that somethings are not worth the mental anguish you're going through. But you'll know when it is worth it. #god #self-love #peace #happiness #growth #rain

self_love_guru7
Clarity is everything to me. Be confident and bold about what you want. If you know you are a high value person don't expect anything less. No time to play games with anyone. #confidence #happiness #peace #selflove #clarity #growth #god #◆

self_love_guru7
Just because I do believe that is 100%. That doesn't mean I'm trying invalidate anything that happened to you being bad. Or life-changing. But this does give you opportunity to stop labeling something that is holding back in life and has you suck there instead of moving forward. Rewatch this a couple times to truly understand what he is saying because if nothing else it is very freeing. #peace #happiness #love #selflove #healthy #god #think #about #it

self_love_guru7
Continue to be happy in the face of miserable people, Who you are holds more weight than anything that these people can do to you. Keep your spirits up keep your positivity and ignore anything else outside of that. Keep your peace. And remember nothing can break you. #peace #selflove #happiness #beyourself #god #is #always #here #for #me #grow

self_love_guru7
Being alone is something that most people see is a bad thing. Somebody even told me once that they don't like to Go out to eat if someone's not going with them. It's like you have to get comfortable with

yourself because one day you never know if you're gonna have to cut off everybody that you thought were close to you. Because people change ,situations change, you change. And not everyone is there for that change. Meaning that they're probably not happy for you because you're elevating in any kind of way. Which is why it is very important to look around you and see who is actually happy for you when good things happen and who is it. But most important you need to be comfortable with being alone and talking to you sometimes. Honestly I have the best conversations with me and you can to. #selflove #peace #happiness #comment #conversation #growth #positivequotes

self_love_guru7

If I do decide to have any children later on I would teach them self-love daily, I would teach them that healing is a daily thing as well, I would teach them to be who they are no matter who is around even if it's "weird" . I would teach that they can do absolutely anything and never let anyone tell you that you can't. And the final and most important thing never allow anyone to make your heart cold because they didn't know how to handle someone with a good heart. #god #be #you #lovequotes #loveyourself #selflove #know #your #worth #powerful #beyond #madetomeasure #happiness #peace

self_love_guru7

Just listening to her be herself and not have to bring down a person that says something negative to her. But instead inform her without giving away her peace or too much of herself. Was beautiful. She was just so soft spoken ,kind and honest. You can see that she has a beautiful soul just though this. I swear when I watched this I was like "HEY GOD BRING ME ONE LIKE THIS"😁. But In all seriousness this is how I Strive to be and you should too◇#beautiful #soul #good #woman #god #healthylifestyle #peace #h piness #goodnight #light #love #selflove #loveyourself #gorgeous #wife #growth #amazing #◇ #◇ #◇ #◇ #☺

self_love_guru7
This is something that I feel like isn't talked about enough and more people need to be aware of this. The way that a person loves they are going to show you. When you first start dating ,talking or whatever you wanna call it. And when they do show you. you need to believe them. Instead of trying to change it. A person is only going to change their behavior if they want to and they see that it is necessary. Often times people feel like that they can tell someone this is what I want because you say that you love me these are things that I want to be shown to feel like I am loved. And there is nothing wrong with sitting down and having a conversation I'm just letting you know now that it's not gonna change the way that they treat you. this person has grown up and been shown love in a certain way and nine times out of 10 the way this person's version of what they were taught love is , It's something that has been hardwired into them since they were young. Now it is your choice to choose if you want to participate in this love that they are giving you. But do not accept less than what you are worth. Love doesn't mean the same to everyone. And I'm not saying that you are not enough for them to change. It's just that this is all that they are capable of giving you because this is all that they are capable of giving themselves. And nobody can love you more than they love themselves-Dae #selflove #happiness #loveyourself #knowyourworth #postivevibes #honesty #growthmind

self_love_guru7
You are human. Sometimes your heart does hurt. Pretending like it doesn't it's just going to hurt you even more. You need to be honest with yourself about how you feel and what you can do to manage those feelings. Crying is usually a way to Alleviate

pain. Exercising or anything else that you may need to do in order to take the stress off. Anything that you need to do to make you feel better no matter who is watching is what you need to do. Do what's best for you. #god #happiness #beyou #beyourownboss #wakeup #hello #girl #gym #peace #positivity #light #try #❤ #◈ #giveaway #loveislove #selflove #foll
self_love_guru7
Having pure intentions with everything you do in life is something that will always put you in a better place mentally, physically, and just in general you'll be happier. Good things will start to pour into your life when you choose peace and self love and genuine intentions go along with that. #❤ #goodmorning #selflove #love #life #peace #happiness #choose #mov

CPSIA information can be obtained
at www.ICGtesting.com
Printed in the USA
BVHW010809150123
656267BV00049B/330